Science Technology Engineering Math
STEM STARTERS FOR KIDS

ASTRONOMY
ACTIVITY
Book

Activities about Space, Planets, and Stars

Written by Jenny Jacoby

Designed and illustrated by Vicky Barker

FOR YOUNG READERS

Visit our website at
www.skyhorsepublishing.com.

10 9 8 7 6 5 4 3 2 1

Design and art direction by Vicky
Barker
Additional illustrations by The
Boy Fitz Hammond

Manufactured in China,
June 2023
This product conforms to
CPSIA 2008

ISBN:
978-1-63158-725-2

WHAT IS ASTRONOMY?

Astronomy is the study of space and everything in it. That includes our planet, Earth. Astronomers use powerful telescopes to observe and measure the stars and planets. They ask questions about how and why everything in space behaves as it does. Studying space can help us to understand more about what makes Earth special. It can also give us clues about how the universe began.

WHAT IS STEM?

STEM stands for "science, technology, engineering and mathematics." These four areas are closely linked, and astronomers use all of them to help in their studies. All astronomers need some STEM knowledge, as they ask big questions about the universe that different STEM skills can help them answer.

Science

Technology

Engineering

Math

WHAT IS SPACE?

Once you travel up and out of Earth's atmosphere, you enter space. It is the vast darkness of the universe! Most of space is empty, with huge distances between stars and planets. Stars give off light that travels across space until it hits something. When you look at the starry night sky, you are seeing light that has traveled through empty space for many years before reaching your eyes.

Where does space begin?
We say that space begins at the Kármán line, which is 62.1 miles (100 km) above the surface of Earth. It is a line marking the change from Earth's blue atmosphere to the darkness of space.

There are all sorts of things in space. Can you find:

Answers on page 30.

5 satellites

6 red stars

3 distant galaxies

2 comets

1 planet with an asteroid belt

THE BIG BANG

The Big Bang is the name for how scientists believe the universe began. It happened almost 14 billion years ago! We don't know what set it off, but within just a few seconds the universe went from being very small, hot, and thick to expanding out in all directions at once.

The bigger the universe grew in those first few seconds, the cooler it got. All that hot energy started to form into tiny particles called **quarks.** After a few minutes, the quarks grouped together into atoms.

The building blocks of the universe we know today were all created in the Big Bang. However, it took millions more years for light, stars, and galaxies to form—and billions of years before our Sun and solar system came into being.

BIG BANG

Quarks

Atoms

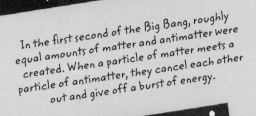

In the first second of the Big Bang, roughly equal amounts of matter and antimatter were created. When a particle of matter meets a particle of antimatter, they cancel each other out and give off a burst of energy.

In this cloud of particles, draw a circle around each pair of matter and antimatter particles.
How many bursts of energy have you created?
What is left over when you have made as many pairs as possible?

matter   antimatter

Answer on page 30.

7

WHAT IS IT LIKE IN SPACE?

Space is a near-perfect **vacuum,** which means it contains very little matter. There is no air to breathe. There is almost no atmospheric pressure or gravity, so things float about and keep moving in one direction until they bump into something. It is very cold, even near the Sun, as there is so little matter to keep the Sun's warmth close to you. Space is full of **radiation,** which can damage the eyes and skin. It is a dangerous place for people to be, as we are adapted to survive inside Earth's atmosphere.

The **visor** protects the face from the Sun's harmful rays.

People cannot survive in space without wearing a spacesuit. A spacesuit surrounds the astronaut's body and provides oxygen to breathe. It also keeps them warm and protects them from radiation.

The **life support pack** powers the spacesuit and provides water to cool the body. It also supplies fresh oxygen to breathe, and removes carbon dioxide.

The **tether** keeps the astronaut from floating out into space when working outside a spacecraft.

An inner layer has tubes for water sewn into it, to keep the body at the right temperature.

Spacesuits are vital for astronauts to wear out in space. How would you decorate your spacesuit? Color in this one.

OUR SOLAR SYSTEM

Our solar system is a collection of eight planets that **orbit** the Sun, a massive star in the center. The Sun pulls things towards it through the force of gravity. This force keeps each planet traveling on its own path, about the same distance from the Sun, and never crashing into any other planet.

The eight planets in our solar system are all different. Some are small; others are big. Some are rocky; others are gassy. The ones closer to the Sun are hotter, and those further away are colder. Our planet, Earth, is the third closest. It is sometimes called "the Goldilocks planet" because it isn't too hot or too cold, but just right for life to exist.

The solar system also includes other objects orbiting the Sun, such as moons, dwarf planets, asteroids, and comets.

MARS

EARTH

VENUS

MERCURY

SUN

Orbit means to travel around something.

URANUS

SATURN

NEPTUNE

JUPITER

Can you make up your own way of remembering the order of the planets? Just think up words that begin with each of these first letters and try to make it make sense. It can be silly!

Pluto isn't actually a planet — it's a dwarf planet!

Want a way to remember the order of the planets in our solar system? Take the first letter of each planet, in order, and make a new saying that is easier to remember. Here is one:

Mercury .... My

Venus .... Very

Earth .... Easy

Mars .... Method

Jupiter .... Just

Saturn .... Speeds

Uranus .... Up

Neptune .... Naming

M _____

V _____

E _____

M _____

J _____

S _____

U _____

N _____

11

WHAT IS A PLANET?

There are lots of different objects in our solar system. Astronomers decide together how we tell these objects apart. A planet is something large and round that orbits a star on a clear path. In our solar system, that star is the Sun.

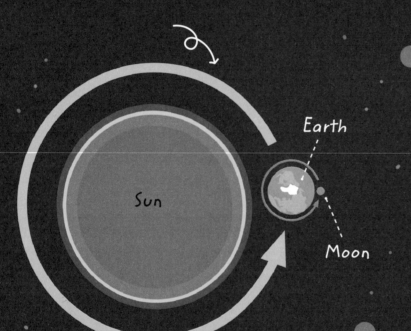

Earth

Sun

Moon

The Moon is not a planet because it orbits a planet (Earth) rather than a star. Some other planets have their own moons—Mars has two, called Phobos and Deimos.

Planets must have strong enough gravity to develop their rounded shape, and to clear any other objects from the path they travel around their star. Astronomers say planets have to be large because the bigger an object is, the more gravity it has to pull things towards it.

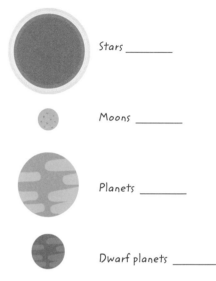

There are planets, moons, and dwarf planets in this busy part of the night sky. Count how many there are of each. Answers on page 30.

Stars _____

Moons _____

Planets _____

Dwarf planets _____

In our solar system, there are dwarf planets as well as planets. Like planets, **dwarf planets** are rounded and orbit the Sun. However, their smaller size makes their gravity too weak to clear their path around the Sun.

Changing definitions

When astronomers discovered Pluto in 1930, they thought it was the ninth planet in our solar system. Over the years, however, astronomers learned more and used more powerful telescopes. In 2006, they decided to create a new category: dwarf planet. Pluto is one of five known dwarf planets in our solar system.

ROCKY, GASSY, AND ICY

There are three types of planet in our solar system: rocky, gassy, and icy planets. Closest to the Sun are the four **rocky** planets: Mercury, Venus, Earth, and Mars. The next two planets, Jupiter and Saturn, are **gas giants.** The furthest planets from the Sun, Uranus, and Neptune, are **ice giants.**

Mercury, Venus, and Mars are all **rocky** like Earth, but are much smaller than Earth.

The **gas giants** are much bigger than Earth. Jupiter is the biggest planet in the solar system. The gas giants might have solid cores (we don't know for sure), but their surface is made of the gases hydrogen and helium.

Can you find the names of all the planets (and the star) of our solar system in this word search? Words can read backwards, forwards, up, down, and diagonally.

MERCURY   MARS   URANUS

VENUS   JUPITER   NEPTUNE

EARTH   SATURN   SUN

Answers on page 31.

The **ice giants** have a solid core and a thick, foggy surface made from water, methane, and ammonia. Orbiting so far from the Sun, these planets are cool enough for their gases to thicken and turn liquid.

```
C A O X M Y D E O H V U V
P S I L E E S G I U V E V
L E N S R H T R A E N A N
P Y T A C D A P T A C T C
E V I D E J U P I T E R T
N S I S A T H S U M H T H
E E L S R V E R L F Q A E
P F M F A D P E M B A I Y
T D U H L T N D U O R L R
U S S L O N U S S L T P U
N E L G N R I R L D S O C
E G L M A P N G N R Q F R
N N E N T X W N E N L E E
A A U Z Z E A A I O U R M
O S T V E N U S T E Y C Y
C W S E E X E C N E K J K
V M T A R S A U T F X A R
A A I M C E S A I O U R U
C R T A A M G O T E Y C Y
O S B R E N L P R M D E N
```

WHAT IS A STAR?

If you have looked into the night sky on a dark, cloudless night, you will know that stars are twinkling bright lights way out in space. There is also one star you can see in the daytime (if it's not too cloudy): the Sun.

The stars in the night sky are just the same as the Sun. Some are bigger, some are smaller, but they are all much further away. This is why they all look smaller than the Sun.

All stars are bright and shining because they are so hot and busy with huge chemical reactions that give off an enormous amount of light. The light travels through space until it reaches Earth, where you can see it.

A star's life

A star is born in a "star nursery" (see page 19). It gets hotter as it grows bigger. Eventually, it gets so hot that it starts to burn, turning hydrogen atoms into helium atoms.

When the hydrogen atoms have all been burned off, the star's heat starts to burn helium, turning it into other elements such as carbon, oxygen, and nitrogen. When a star has used up all its fuel, it can explode in a supernova—which is so powerful that it can outshine billions and billions of stars put together.